RUBBER
Chickens
FOR THE SOUL

**BAD
DOG
PARODY**

Bad Dog Press
P.O. Box 130066
Roseville, MN 55113

e-mail: badogpress@aol.com & badogbook@aol.com

Rubber Chickens for the Soul

First printed in 1996

Printed in the United States of America.
96 97 98 99 00   5 4 3 2 1

Text: Tim Nyberg, Tony Dierckins, and Scott Pearson

Special thanks to Jake Nyberg for "Grandpa's Legacy" and "Missing an Old Friend" and to Bob Stromberg for "Keep the Ram in Your Rama-lama-ding-dong."

ISBN 1-887317-03-1
Library of Congress Catalog Card Number: 95-83150

Warning: Contains humor, a highly volatile substance if used improperly. Harmful if swallowed. All content is a fictional product of the authors' imaginations. Any resemblance between characters portrayed herein and actual persons living, dead, or residing in New Jersey is purely coincidental. Contents under pressure. Do not use near open flame. Do not use as a flotation device, or at least avoid any situations in which you would need to rely on a book as a flotation device. All typographic errors are purely intentional and left for your amusement. Always say no to drugs and, by all means, stay in school.

CONTENTS

Contents, continued

INTRODUCTION

The authors of the hilariously disturbing stories in this book aren't famous writers. None of them have ever worked as humorists, comics, or television weather personalities. Nor are they inspirational speakers called upon to translate their wit and wisdom to the printed page. Rarely have they worked the keyboards of typewriters, word processors, or personal computers. In fact, most of them shouldn't operate heavy equipment while using the kind of medication it takes to keep them lucid.

So who wrote these stories, you ask, these "rubber chickens for the soul"?

Well, our contributors would just as soon not reveal their identity. Many of them, you see, created their work as part of a therapy program. As you read, you will undoubtedly notice that quite a few of the authors still have a long, long way to go to recovery. Some consider their lives works in progress; others, rough drafts or simply outlines; a couple are still having trouble coming up with a topic. Furthermore, they fear that when they have successfully emerged from the veil of whatever misfortune has inspired their current muse, they very well may not appreciate, let alone wish to be associated with, some of the ideas expressed herein.

This is, of course, a parody of those *Chicken Soup for the Soul* books, and we've tried to include stories from each of the categories they use. Fans of *Chicken Soup* will recognize that we haven't included any "Loving Yourself" stories. We felt this category would be, well, too obvious. Besides, everyone needs a hobby.

We welcome you to a celebration of the dysfunctional, 33 ⅓ gut-wrenching tales taken from the intersection where inspiration collides with desperation to turn even the best of attitudes to roadkill. We present them here to tickle your funny bone, to challenge your perception of acceptable good taste, and to make you stop and say to yourself, "Good God, this is pathetic; I guess my life's pretty good after all."

So if your soul's had enough *Chicken Soup* to make you sick, we hope our collection of rubber chickens helps to cleanse your palate.

— The Editors of Bad Dog Press

Love

〜

THE ONE THAT GOT AWAY

*I*t was the first day of fifth grade when she walked into the classroom and turned my life completely upside down. Neither I nor anyone else snuggled safely within the walls of Mrs. Maywell's room—housed inside the hallowed halls of Bluffwood Falls Elementary deep in the Wisconsin heartland—had ever seen anything like her.

Her long, dark brown, almost black hair hung to the small of her back and framed her gloriously oval face. Her brown skin shone in brilliant contrast against the white peasant blouses she wore nearly every day of the week, and her milk chocolate eyes melted the very souls of every one of us pasty-white scandahoovian boys and turned our ashen, pinched-faced sisters pale green with the monster of envy. Yes, when Consuela Martinez moved to Bluffwood Falls, my life would never be the same.

I was in love. Yet, no matter how hard I tried to get her attention, it was clear that Consuela didn't even know I was alive. I snuck little gifts into her desk. I called her at home, but hung up whenever someone answered, never having the nerve to speak. I went out of my way to hit her when we played dodge ball. Nothing worked.

Then came the saddest day of my young life. The teacher announced that Consuela's father had finally raised enough money to fix the truck, and the Martinez family would soon be off chasing harvests in warmer climes. Consuela said goodbye to the classroom, waving with a closed fist as she walked out of the room. I could hear the timbers of my heart fail under the weight of her departure, but as she passed my little desk her fist opened, and there, in orange marker, were the words "I Love You."

I never saw Consuela Martinez again, and many times since I have thought back on that time and wondered what might have been—how my life might have been different had her father found full-time work in Bluffwood Falls. I've also thought back and asked myself if my memory was accurate. Did she really appear as angelic as I remember? Maybe she didn't wear peasant blouses all the time. Perhaps her hair wasn't all that close to being black. She may, in fact, have been a redhead. And now that I think about it, I'm pretty sure her dad was a UPS driver and they moved after he got a transfer to Kenosha. And it probably wasn't orange marker. To be honest, whoever it was never even wrote any message for me on her hand. Really, there's a good chance I made the whole thing up or maybe read it somewhere or heard someone else tell a story like that. Could even be that I was thinking about Gretta Olsen. She had red hair.

No matter. Even if it was just the Olsen girl, I'll always remember Consuela Martinez as the one that got away.

A NEW YEAR'S RESOLUTION
FOR SINGLE PERSONS

I refuse to accept that love has left my life just because I'm single. Therefore, I vow to stop feeling "lonely" and "sexually frustrated" (if not downright inadequate) by redefining my concept of self in order to render these terms meaningless and inapplicable to my state of being.

To this end, I hereby recognize that I am asexual, much like the one-celled creatures found in a drop of pond water; as a direct consequence of this, I also state unequivocally that my private parts are vestigial organs, not unlike the appendix.

Therefore, if ever I am in a position demanding surgery anywhere near my groinular region, I shall instruct the doctor to remove the aforementioned privates as long as he or she is in the neighborhood.

Nevertheless I shall continue to look forward to the possibility of reproduction, recognizing that at virtually any moment I could spontaneously divide into two genetically identical human beings. Until such time, however, I will continue to perceive my singular existance as not only natural, but preferred, and recognize that the love within me is not only whole, but pure.

I wish myself a happy New Year!

It Is Better . . .

*I*t is better to have loved and lost
than to have had your heart
ripped out and shoved in
your face while it's
still beating.

*A*ctually, if you to think about it,
just about anything is better than
having your heart ripped out,
even if whoever does the ripping
decides *not* to shove it in your face
while it's still beating.

THE WOMAN OF MY DREAMS WAS NAMED EDINA BARBER

I'll never forget the first time I saw Edina Barber. Unless I'm hit on the head like Uncle Morton, who thinks he's a bobsled. Every time it snows he wants to be pushed down the street on his back. It would be fun if only he could take corners. Please, Morty, would it kill you to bank just a little?

Anyhow, Tuesday, September 20, 1955, seventh grade, a hush falls over the lunchroom as the new girl walks in at six minutes past noon. She seems to glide along in slow motion, her hair moving as if in a summer breeze. Her thin sweater clings to precocious curves, a pleated skirt dancing above her knees. The boys smile, the girls frown, even the teachers look uncomfortable. Forty years later and it's still like it's happening right before my eyes, except now I'm wearing this truss, thanks for reminding me.

Then a cloud passes over the sun and the lunchroom lights seem to focus only on her. She blushes, just a little, smiles, then nervously wets her full lips with a slow twirl of her tongue. A sigh moves through the boys, clinging in their throats like sudden humidity or maybe a big lump of cream cheese melting off a toasted bagel. Billy Gupkin, overcome with desire and frustration, vomits into his lunchbox. Then it happens. She turns toward me. The light on her shines my way, suddenly I'm the moon and she's the sun. I smile like a crazy man let out of a straitjacket. I'm blinded by her face, I let my eyes fall away, rushing down her body to the floor like a barrel over Niagara Falls.

And that's when I see Edina Barber, the other new girl, her uneven feet in last year's Keds stretch out on gangly legs into the path of the glowing beauty who favors me with her blue-eyed glance. I start to call out, but too late, my voice cracks under the strain, and the goddess trips over Edina Barber, pitches forward, her beauty somehow, unbelievably, enhanced by the fear that crosses her face as she falls to the floor. Her pleated skirt turns inside out over her waist, revealing legs disappearing into white cotton underpants with pink flowers. Several boys get spontaneous nose bleeds, but I only have eyes for Edina Barber, who leans forward with a smirk on her face and evil in her heart.

Six years later I married the girl with the flowered underpants, but Edina Barber was the woman haunting me as I worked in my father's discount bomb shelter factory to support my transcendent wife. Edina Barber, just the name itself like a bitter honey in my mouth. I will never forget her, Edina Barber, the woman of my dreams, the woman that showed me what true love really was.

Parenting

~

What My Father Told Me

*T*here comes a time in life when a person is old enough to know that they don't know everything, yet young enough that they still go to their parents for help. For me it happened shortly after my sixteenth birthday. I had my driver's permit and was anxious to get a car of my own, but knew I'd have to get a job because times were tough and Mom couldn't work on account of her babies. Looking back now I realize her "babies" were just shiny things she found on the road-side, but back then it seemed important, and those were simpler times.

Since I needed some guidance as I made this tran-sition into adult life, I got up early one morning to meet Dad as he got home from the graveyard shift at the sheep mill, before he took his sleep medicine that he brewed himself in the basement from table scraps. I pulled up a chair at the kitchen table as he struggled out of his work slippers, and asked him what I should do with my life.

He took a deep breath, then slowly exhaled. "Son," he said, leaning closer to me. "I just got one thing to say. Never go to the can on your break. Always go on company time. It's the only time in your life you'll get paid to drop a load off, unless you're like your weird cousin Epsom, who sells his bodily functions for medical experiments. And, believe you me, you don't want to be like him."

He sat back in his chair and suddenly looked nervous. Staring out the window, he continued. "Oh, yeah, well, about women. If someone says they're uncomfortable doing something with you, you know, in bed, don't just go and get them another pillow. That's probably not what they mean. Instead, remain calm, take off your costume, and move slowly away from the bed with your hands in the air." He cleared his throat, then without looking at me, shuffled into the basement.

That was the last time I saw Dad, because his still exploded and rendered him invisible. At least that's what Mom told me. Looking back now I realize that was probably just her way of saying he had run out on us under cover of the resulting fire. Nevertheless, to this day I remember his last words to me, and look forward to the time I'll be able to pass the family wisdom on to my own son. My only regret is Dad isn't here to help me blow up anything.

☙

I'm No Mike Brady

I never really thought of myself as a good father. Caring, perhaps, and diligent. I tried hard. But not good. Not in a Mike-Brady-willing-to-adopt-three-daughters-just-to-knock-boots-with-Florence-Henderson kind of way. I don't think I have that kind of patience. I certainly don't make the kind of money to support six kids, a live-in cook/maid, and a stay-at-home wife. And I could never get my hair to curl like that, not even with the help of a Toni Home Permanent and the humidity of a rain forest. And Lord knows I've tried.

No, I considered myself just an OK dad, but not a good one. It seemed to me I was always a step behind in my son's interests. The Sega Genesis I picked up didn't have enough "bits" to play the games Billy played at the neighbor's house. When I came home with a hand-stitched Brazilian soccer ball, he was gazing at in-line skates in the Sears Christmas catalog. And when I finally accepted the Barbie thing, Billy had already moved on to G.I. Joe.

"That's OK, Dad," he'd always say in that patronizing tone of his. "Thanks." He'd play with whatever I'd brought home for a few minutes, but as soon as I left the room, he'd set it aside, and by the next day the gift I thought he wanted so dearly found itself among the growing pile of discarded playthings that overflowed his closet. What kind of father was I, I asked myself, who couldn't even buy his son's love and respect when retail stores sat stuffed with the means?

"That's OK." The words stung me. Time and time again, he'd tell me it was "OK," but I knew it wasn't. It's tough for a kid. Kids judge other kids by their stuff, and Billy's mom and I couldn't afford to keep up with the trends, even though we both worked. The raises down at the slaughterhouse weren't coming as fast as they once did, Gwen was only getting in about twenty-five hours a week at the electrolysis clinic, and with us helping with her mother's methadone treatment, we barely made ends meet. But I wasn't going to let that stop me from being a good father.

After I learned Billy could care less about Power Rangers, I dedicated myself to finding the perfect gift. He was fourteen, and I'd heard enough "It's OK, Dad; thanks" to last me a lifetime. I researched: I scoured the latest journals of early teen psychology to figure out what he was thinking; I subscribed to Japanese business magazines and hired an interpreter to stay abreast, if not ahead, of the latest trends in toys and games; I secretly listened in on his phone calls to friends; I hid in the playground to watch him and the other boys play. And despite that little "stalking" misunderstanding with the park police, I started to learn a lot about my son and the interests of a boy his age.

After several months, a plan began to gel. I plotted. I calculated. I even opened a separate savings account to cover costs. Within a year I not only discovered the perfect gift for my soon-to-be-fifteen-year-old son, but would have enough cash to cover it and pick up a bottle of Harvey's Bristol Cream so the wife and I could celebrate my inevitable success.

The night of Billy's birthday finally arrived, and instead of taking my usual route home, I stopped at an ATM and took out enough cash for his present, drove the back streets to an unfamiliar part of town, procured the gift, then headed the station wagon to the

Fourteenth Street trestle where I knew I would find Billy and his friends smoking cigarettes and throwing rocks at the trains. Ah, sweet innocence of youth!

I stepped out of the car, waved "hello" to my son, opened the passenger door, and helped a certain Miss "Whoever-You'd-Like-Me-to-Be" to her feet.

"Son," I said, trying not to tear up. "She's all yours—at least for an hour. Happy birthday."

Billy's face beamed; his friends just stared in amazement. I'd never seen anyone look so happy in my life, except maybe my cousin Julius after he had his wisdom teeth removed, and even then once the pain killers wore off he turned back into his miserable self.

"Wow!" Billy exclaimed. "Thanks, Dad. You're the greatest!"

I admit I felt pretty darn pleased with myself. I'll also have to admit that the gift didn't sit too well with everyone. Gwen, in particular, had a little problem with the whole idea, and that may very well be why she left me. I don't know. I guess we'll find out during the taping of "Jenny Jones."

Maybe I'm not exactly Mike Brady. But then again, how smart was he? He was supposed to be an architect, yet he crammed nine people and a dog into a four-bedroom house. He had no right to whine when Greg wanted to turn the den into his own private bachelor pad.

It's true, I'm no Mike Brady. But I am Billy's dad, and to him I'm more than just OK. I'm the greatest.

I Don't Agree . . .

I don't agree with that old proverb, "Children are better seen than heard," especially if you're in a really dark room. In which case, I find it easier to hear them.

Either way, watch your step and remember this: I would have gotten away with it if not for those meddling kids!

GRANDPA'S LEGACY

I was almost five when grandpa came to live with us. He was already older than old, but I didn't mind, because he was a jolly, easygoing guy. It was nice to have Mom's dad around the house, especially with my dad on the road delivering acorns to needy squirrels, a seasonal humanitarian effort which kept him away for months at a time. Grandpa had a lot of wisdom to share, and remained talkative well into his later, "Did I ever tell you about the time I dated Amelia Earhart?" years. He quickly became like a second father to me.

The first thing I noticed about Grandpa was the strange odor that followed him around. It was like nothing I had ever smelled, an awful mix of compost and latex. In that innocent way kids have, I asked him, "Woo! What got sick and died in your shorts?"

"It's my magic pants," he told me. "And the smell is a small price to pay for the powers they give me."

Well, that was good enough for me. I loved him

dearly despite his stench, and I never told him what I thought of the awful odor that wafted about him. But I wondered how he could stand his own reek. I tried dropping little hints, and even made him a necklace out of a whole forest of pine tree air fresheners, but it didn't help. He still smelled terrible.

So I tried my best to overcome the obstacle between us and spent many hours by Grandpa's side, soaking in his years of wisdom. He taught me to fish and to tie flies, and along the way I learned a lot about life and to find humor in adverse situations. Those summer days knee-deep in trout streams were the best of my life, as the outdoor breezes and the added layer of Grandpa's waders kept the unfortunate odor away and pulled us even closer. Of course, that might have been the current.

Eventually he became very ill, and called me to his deathbed. His voice had grown feeble, so I bent down close to his face to hear him whisper his final words of wisdom. He tried to clear his throat to speak, but as he did the breath that escaped him over-whelmed me. It made the magic pants seem like a warm breeze after a summer rain. It struck my senses with such force that I jerked back, my nose and eyes stinging at the foul stench. Tears blurred my vision, and as I flailed around blindly for a towel, I accidentally hooked his IV tube, pulling it from his arm. By the time I could see, it was too late. Grandpa was dead. His doctors said it wasn't my fault; his time had come. This consoled me little: Grandpa died without telling me his final wishes.

As I dressed for his funeral, Mother handed me a box. "He wanted you to have these," she said. The smell told me what I'd find in the box, so I just unfolded the note taped to the cover: "I'm not really incontinent. I just loves to wear them magic pants." Mother and I laughed until we cried: it was just like Grandpa to give us laughter in the face of despair.

They say a person's children are her or his legacy. Grandpa didn't have any boys, and like I said, I thought of him as my second father. As his legacy, I try always to keep his spirit alive. No matter what anybody says, I'm going to keep wearing those magic pants.

∾

Learning & Teaching

WHEN THE TEACHER BECOMES THE STUDENT

They say in any successful person's past is a teacher who stood out, who facilitated a turning point in the student's life. For example, Elmer Bumper, the famous tourniquet magnate, often tells the story of his second grade gym teacher, Mr. Gruntle, who repeatedly put Elmer in a headlock for soiling himself during dodgeball. In fact, Elmer never shuts up about Mr. Gruntle, often just shouting "Gruntle!" over and over until his throat bleeds. They also say that people who sell tourniquets often have a high percentage of "friends" who do little to curb behavior that causes excessive bleeding of the throat.

While stories like Elmer's make it obvious that teachers have a tremendous impact on their students, we often forget the reverse, that students can influence their teachers as well. They say the best teachers welcome such two-way relationships with their children. Mrs. Argyle Phrufru of Loose Stitch Elementary School has taught kindergarten for eighty years, and at one hundred and three years young, attributes her youthfulness to her students.

"Oh, yes, the happy innocence of my kids has had an enormous impact on me. It makes you remember the truly important things in life. Why, just the other day, I was feeling a little down. I was troubled by Hume's assault on the self. I wanted to simply accept Descartes's 'I think therefore I am' without skepticism, but Hume's notion of ideas as ever changing seemed to eliminate the possibility of a constant self.

"Luckily little Tommy Widget came up to me and showed me that life's too short for such worries. He looked up at me with a smile on his face and held out a small bouquet of wildflowers he had picked for me on the way to school. It was a bright spring day and his twinkling blue eyes were filled with the hope that melting snow brings. 'Mrs. Phrufru,' he said in his soft, shy voice. 'Hume's chief problem in denying the self was an inability to clearly define his alternative. The mere "bundle of perceptions" metaphor he posits falls apart under the slightest semantic pressure. The *World Book Dictionary* defines "bundle" as "a number of things tied or wrapped together." Surely the tie that bundles our perceptions together is nothing other than the Cartesian self.' Then he wiped his nose on his shirt sleeve and I told him to use a tissue. It just made my whole day."

They say you can't teach an old dog new tricks, but can you ever really be too old to learn, or too young to teach? It's the simple naivete of children that can be so helpful to a cynical adult. What does Mrs. Phrufru have to say about it?

"I'm just going to go on teaching and learning until they pry my kids from my cold dead fingers."

NOW THAT I KNOW ABOUT "BABY" CORN

*T*he whole concept of those little "baby" ears of corn used to bother me. It made me sick to think of corn trying to grow in tiny, confining spaces while being force-fed veal. Never allowed to roam free and wave in the wind like the other ears. Never realizing their potential.

But my anxieties and disapproval of baby corn ranching methods were born of ignorance. I had based my feelings on misinformation.

After my ranting on one night about the evils of vegetable moguls growing fat off the misery of suffering infant ears, a friend of mine explained that what I thought was going on wasn't the case at all. "Baby" corn, she explained, was created using the same process so-called primitive South American tribes use to shrink heads.

With the truth, my friend liberated my ill feelings. She taught me about baby corn, but she also taught me that it's usually best to get the facts before writing a bunch of letters to the editor.

She did something more for me. You see, it warmed my heart to think that good old U.S. of A. American corn could be adapted by a South American process in order to enhance oriental stir-fry recipes.

Now, when someone mentions "world peace" I just smile and think to myself, *It's possible. In this world, it's possible.*

All I Ever Need to Know . . .

A wise man once said:
"All I ever need to know,
I learned in kindergarten."

This, of course, would explain
why I get so crabby if meetings
encroach on my nap time.

JUST SAY "NO," DOROTHY

*A*mericans love the *Wizard of OZ*. The enchanting tale of a girl who learns there's no place like home has become part of the American tapestry. Like cotton, it is interwoven with the lessons of childhood—the very fabric of our lives. As an adult, however, I find that each annual viewing raises my anxiety for the America I live in, and I fear it may be teaching our children lessons just as dangerous as those taught by gangsta rap, talk radio, and the subversive subtext of "The Golden Girls." I've come to the conclusion that the *Wizard of OZ* is not the innocent dreamscape we all love, but an unresolved story that glamorizes drug use and violence.

Shameless drug promotion runs throughout the film. As Dorothy and her pals clear the woods with Emerald City in their sights, the Wicked Witch of the

West puts them to sleep. Her method? Poppies. When plastic, these little red flowers make fine V.F.W. lapel pins; in their organic state, however, they make opium. Baked out of their brains, Dorothy and her crew crash hard, passing out in a field of flowers and foreshadowing the summer of '68.

They are saved by Glinda, the Good Witch of the North. But what is it this "good" witch uses to release them from their narcotic slumber? Snow—a not-so-clever street name for cocaine. Our favorite clan of misfits awake wired to the gills on blow and sing as they skip merrily down the canary-colored path to find refuge in the Emerald City, where they indulge in the sensual pleasures of rubdowns and makeovers and enjoy psychedelic visions of a horse that changes hue.

They have found a temporary escape, but what type of life awaits them further down the yellow brick road? Glinda and the Wicked Witch have started our heroes on a destructive cycle of using opiates and stimulants to get them through the day. They are merely running to the shelter of mother's little helper, taking a little something to relax and a little something to wake up. Not exactly a healthy lesson, yet we celebrate this film and watch it with our kids while we lock out MTV so they don't hear about the Chronic from Dr. Dre and other musicians who may be facing criminal charges.

Besides promoting drugs, the film's technicolor dream sequence is littered with violence. During their adventure, our heroes are pelted with apples, chased, set aflame, and even torn apart by flying monkeys. They also assault a trio of Ajax-complected castle guards and liquefy the Wicked Witch of the West (whose sister died after being struck by a farm house so hard that she fell not merely dead, but really quite sincerely dead—a violent act that causes an entire village of short extras to break out in song). But why are they on this dangerous journey? Is it necessary?

Well, no. After Dorothy and her pals experience a bounty of drugs and violence, Glinda tells the farm girl she has had the power to go home all along—the ruby slippers. Yet Glinda forces the gang into situations whose only resolve comes through violence—the same reason parents' organizations hurl criticism at TV shows like "Power Rangers." Good witch, indeed.

So does her journey really teach Dorothy that there's no place like home? I think not. Consider the story's central conflict (it's not returning to Kansas—that's all just a dream). Dorothy runs away, comes back too late to find shelter, gets hit on the noggin, and whisks away to dreamland because Old Lady Gulch has a police order to have Toto put to death: it seems that wacky little dog has been raiding her garden, a canine crime presumably punishable by death in 1930s Kansas. Ah, the land of *E Pluribus Unum*.

So when Dorothy claims "There's no place like home," the lesson doesn't ring true. She may be safe at home in her black and white world, but she always has been. Gulch still has that order. Toto—Toto too—is toast. After her psychedelic journey, Dorothy is stuck with the same problem she had before—and a big ol' headache to boot. Perhaps that's the true lesson: "You can't run away from your problems"—you can't hide from reality behind a gauzy veil of narcotics or expect violence to solve your problems, not without causing yourself greater pain or at least a hangover.

The Wizard of Oz squanders an opportunity to teach valuable lessons. Home's nice, but tell that to the homeless or the countless hordes from dysfunctional families. Why not tell us where the red brick road goes? In Munchkin Land, it spirals around the yellow path, but the film ignores it. Perhaps it leads to a better way to solve our problems. Unfortunately, we'll never know. No wonder Judy Garland O.D.'d.

ॐ

Living Your Dream

~

THE LITTLE GIRL WITH A VERY BIG DREAM

There once was a little girl, about four years old, who already knew what her life's dream was. She called it her Very Big Dream, and it filled all her waking thoughts. She told everyone she met her Very Big Dream. During the day she did crayon drawings of the Very Big Dream. At night she wished upon a star that her Very Big Dream would come true. While she slept she dreamed her Very Big Dream in rich colors and minute detail. Every morning when she got up she would run first thing to her parents' bedroom and tell them the Very Big Dream all over again, from start to finish.

"Yes, yes!" her mother would say.

"Oh, it's gonna happen!" her father would say.

Years later, however, after she had fulfilled the Very Big Dream, she remembered their enthusiastic responses and realized that they had just been having sex, which explained that one time her mother had said, "A little slower, and to the left."

Don't Let Others Stop You...

*D*on't let others stop you from living your dream. For they are not you, and they will never know the fire that burns within you.

In fact, not everyone even likes habanero sauce, let alone wants to put it on everything they eat.

KEEP THE 'RAM' IN YOUR RAMA-LAMA-DING-DONG

*W*hen I was thirteen, I heard a song that changed my life. In this lovely tune, the singer describes being awestruck at the sight of a fine, good-looking girl walking down the street "just as natural as can be." He tells us his love for her grew so strong that he not only had to make her his, but that he nearly lost his mind without her. Before we know it, however, he sings with joy because now he and the girl of his dreams walk side by side, hand in hand on their way to his place. He has found true love.

Throughout the ballad, the singer punctuates his narrative with the ever poignant refrain, "Doo-wa-ditty-ditty-dum-ditty-doo." That subtle turn of phrase grabbed me. It told me that nothing—not even finding true love—was out of reach, no dream of mine was unattainable.

When I hear that song today, I sometimes imagine its writer walking the cold, mean streets of London or New York, knocking on doors of heartless record company executives to pitch his song of hope. I imagine him encountering those who don't share his vision and perhaps becoming discouraged when they suggest things like, "No, no—it should be 'Dit-wah-dooey-ditty-wah-dooey-dit.'" Or, "I like the verses, but let's change the refrain to 'Shoo-wah-shuffle-shuffle-shooey-shooey-shup.' You know, because she's shuffling her feet, right?"

But that young songwriter stuck to his guns. He knew the words of the refrain were those the girl sang to herself and, later, those the lovers sang together. She was not aping the sound of her shoes. She wasn't singing "dit-wah-dooey" anything. And because of his persistence, the song came to life as he had imagined it, and since its release it has inspired myself along with a generation of others.

Think of it: what might have happened if he or other songwriters had allowed producers to walk all over them? Would the inspirational theme of "Get a Job" ring as clear without the enthusiasm of its "Shana-na-na, Shana-nana-na-na" chorus? Would the tenor of "Good night, Sweetheart" sound as sweet and sad without the accompanying bass of "Dit-didit-dit-dow"? I think not.

And so I pose to you these simple questions: Who put the "bop" in the bop-shoobop-shoobop? Who put the "ram" in the rama-lama-ding-dong? Gifted souls, no doubt. Women and men of great insight, blessed with the skill to turn a phrase in such a way that it lights the lives of thousands across a restless nation.

I can only look at how I've been blessed and pray, "Thank you, oh Lord, that this songwriter had the courage to hold on to his dream!"

And so I say to you, my friends, live your lives according to your dreams. Shout your "Doo-wah-ditties" from the rooftops. Always keep the ram in your rama-lama-ding-dong.

STALLWORTH DIDDLEY'S DREAM OF THE FUTURE

Stallworth Diddley settled into his great wicker chair, once again awash in the same blissful contentment that embraced the planet. He turned and gave an approving smile to Sheba, his state-appointed partner in eroticism (who recently announced her plans to forgo clothing whenever the kids were out of the house) as she handed him another tall glass of that delightful little concoction that had made possible all the miracles of recent history: a delicate balance of pineapple-orange-banana juice mixed with three fingers of spiced rum and just a whisper of Prozac and psilocybin—the Kaleidoscope Kocktail.

The drink was first introduced at the historic 1998 Perot-Hussein summit and has been credited with putting the wheels in motion that eventually led to world peace, the ecological recovery of the planet, and the elimination of economic imbalances.

Yet with all these advances, he still stopped to ponder what could be: will his recent DNA test indicate that he is, in fact, the last remaining relative of the 1986 inductee to the Rock and Roll Hall of Fame with whom he shared a surname and, therefore, the rightful heir to that fabled collection of square-bodied guitars?

But as Sheba knelt beside him and asked if he had any further needs, if he knew what she meant, the bubble burst: he awoke with his head pounding, his fingers sticky with fruit juice, and his bladder pleading to him for relief. Of course, it was just a dream, and a silly dream at that. But a dream's a dream, and a guy can dream, can't he?

Yes, we should all do our best to live our dream, no matter how much others may laugh.

Overcoming Obstacles

~

At What Cost Blue?

*E*veryone was happy for Edwina, and proud of her, too. After a lengthy "rest" at Redeeming Oaks and extensive medication, she had rejoined society as a contributing member. She found a job and an apartment and had even talked of dating again. Whether all the crimes attributed to her were her fault or, as her lawyer contends, "happy coincidences for the boys in the forensics lab," Edwina was all better now. Yes, we were all overjoyed for Edwina.

Her coming-out party was shaping into a huge

success. All of her old friends were there, and even some new friends from "the inside" as she so endearingly called it. Family, former colleagues, legal counsel—heck, even a couple members of the prosecution team and the judge himself showed up to wish Edwina well and take advantage of the incredible spread her parents put on. She basked in the glow of acceptance and was careful not to drip sauce from those little cocktail wienies on her new dress.

The night went on, the string quartet providing accompaniment to the chiming din of pleasant conversation among happy revelers. Edwina was graceful, almost delicate in the way she moved from guest to guest to thank them for their kindness, careful always to say just the right thing to the right people. It was around nine, when the buffet was cleared and the desserts and other after-dinner treats were laid out, that trouble struck.

Edwina was complimenting the mayor on his recent acquittal when she reached an innocent hand into a crystal bowl filled with M&M candies. As she brought a sweet, round, melt-in-your-mouth-but-not-in-your-hands treat to her mouth, she noticed something different. It was blue. It was a remarkable blue. Darker than royal yet not as overbearing as navy, the new M&M blue practically danced on her fingertips, shimmering its way to her mouth. Excited, Edwina turned to the bowl and started picking through, extracting just the new blue treats and popping one after another into her mouth. Truly, she was now tasting freedom. *Oh*, she thought, *what a world, what a wonderful, glorious world filled with marvelous blue candies where a girl like me can commit brutal atrocities and yet, with the help of the right behavior and enough cash for good attorneys, rejoin the loving embrace of society with just the minor inconvenience of a few months' incarceration and several thousand therapeutic volts of electricity.*

When the blue were gone, she kept eating. First, the warm side of the color wheel: the reds, oranges, the yellows. Then on to the greens—oh those deliciously naughty greens—before gobbling up all the dark browns, and then—

Edwina stopped. There were no more M&Ms in the dish. But something was wrong! She had eaten no light brown candies! Where were the light brown candies?

"No!" she cried out. "God, no! Oh, M&M-Mars, what have you done?" Edwina shouted at the ceiling, shaking her fists in anger. "Sure, the blue is nice. We all like the blue. But why have you abandoned light brown? Why has it been sacrificed? A new color may increase sales, but at what cost? At what cost blue?"

She continued to scream her lament at the loss of the coffee-with-a-little-cream-colored candies lost now except in childhood memories, pulled a small semiautomatic weapon from beneath her gown, and sprayed the room and most of the guests with hot Teflon before taking her own life, somewhat awkwardly, using the ladle from the punch bowl.

"Oh, Edwina," her mother cried later as the authorities finished their investigation. "Look at that carpet. That'll never come out."

The coroner's report would mention the explosive combination of Edwina's antihallucinogenic medication with large amounts of sugar and cocoa. Sadly, however, it never mentioned her reaction to the change in her favorite candies, at least not directly. Edwina had overcome so much and had gone so far, only to have her ambitions dashed by the loss of one of her favorite treats. To this day we still wonder who's really to blame.

❧

Facing Insurmountable Problems

When faced with a seemingly insurmountable problem, you may choose to use a stepladder.

If so, make sure it's a wooden one, because using an aluminum ladder close to power lines is just asking for more trouble.

Oh, and don't use that part of the ladder that says "Not a Step" on it. Believe you me, it's not a step, even though it really looks like one.

WHEN HANDED LEMONS, MAKE QUICHE

*A*nyone can make lemonade from lemons, right? Sure. But you're better than that, more creative, more resourceful. They never thought you'd amount to anything, but you'll show them. Just keep telling yourself that. You know why? Because it's true, that's why. And I should know. You all know who I am, even if you've never met me. My name is Maynard Q. Crinklepoof, and I'm the CEO of Crinklepoof Industries International Incorporated.

Oh, yeah, you've heard of me now, right? Sure, C3I, makers of the Wonder Sausage™, the self-stuffing casing that makes it easy to eat anything in a hot dog bun. Or maybe you're familiar with BeerGel™, the miracle in a tube that turns any brewed beverage into a creamy pudding. You'll never spill another drop of your favorite draught with BeerGel™.

Yes, when I was a lad, they told me I was strange. They told me to act like the other kids. They told me to stop putting rotten fruit in the collection basket. They told me to put my hands up in the air and step away from the gun. Did I listen? No. That's "N" and "O"—no! I wasn't about to be stifled, constricted, limited, straitjacketed, handcuffed, or imprisoned by society's tunnel vision, its preconceived notions of what you can or can't do. Of course, eventually, as you may remember from the extensive media coverage of the time, I was straitjacketed, handcuffed, and imprisoned, but those are only physical limitations. A wall of stone is nothing compared to the power of a creative mind. They haven't yet built the prison that can hold my imagination.

So if years of incarceration, medication, and shock treatment haven't held me back, what's your problem? Let me tell you. You're listening to other people: the nay-sayers, the it-won't-workers, the isn't-that-against-the-lawers, the that's-the-kind-of-idea-that-will-get-your-brain-on-display-in-a-jar-of-formaldehyde-after-you've-been-mercifully-put-down-like-the-sick-animal-you-arers.

Well, forget them. History sure will. But you're different. Your name will be chiseled into monuments right beneath mine. So cancel your subscriptions, quit your job, leave your family, and change your name to something you like. You're coming to work for me. We're going to change the world. I don't care what color you are, what language you speak, what god you pray to for forgiveness after committing something "society" labels a "crime." There's nothing you can't do. Nothing.

Confronting Daunting Tasks

When forced to confront a
daunting task, approach it
cautiously and take small steps,
carefully placing one foot
in front of the other.

Of course, if you're afraid of looking
silly, just walk like you normally
do and pray you don't trip
over anything

YOU'RE NEVER ALONE

After my third husband left me, I'd never felt so alone in my life, except for maybe when my first and second husbands left me, or when my weimaraner, Ed, ran away, or maybe those two weeks when I was eight and my folks disappeared until they "remembered" where we lived. But I guess when Eddie (husband #3) took off with the housekeeper, it was even more painful. She was a live-in, and I knew I'd never find someone that loving and caring who also did windows. Not for what I was paying her, anyway.

I moped around feeling sorry for myself for months on end. Why did they always leave me? Would I ever find true happiness? Must I spend my life alone? Where do we keep the glass cleaner?

It was at this time that Nanna fell ill, and I found

myself spending many of my evenings at the hospital consoling her. Soon, however, it was she who comforted me. I had poured my heart out to her, listing off my losses and fears. She had outlived four husbands and at least one postal carrier.

"If dairies still delivered milk," she always said, "I would have lived a full life."

But as she neared death, her regrets were few, and most involved ordering all those magazines just to stay on the Prize Patrol's mailing list. I, she said, should buck up and look on the bright side.

"All this whining, 'My husband left me; nobody loves me; I'll die alone; blah, blah, blah.' Well, it's all a bunch of hooey," she yelled above the din of her respirator. "You listen to me: you're never alone. No matter where you go or what you do, you're surrounded by mites. Millions and millions of the little buggers. They're in your couch and carpets, your bedding and mattress, your clothes, and all over you! They look like tiny little crabs and they live off the flakes of your dead skin. They've covered you since the moment you were born and every night you sleep nestled in little mite cities and when you die the mites will be setting up permanent housing in that nice navy blue outfit they'll bury you in. Gives me the creeps just thinking about it. No, you're never alone. So just quit your whining, already. You think it's any fun listening to your problems while I lie here helpless with all these tubes sticking out of me?"

Nanna, of course, was right. I've kept her words with me since that day; and last Saturday, as I waited at the altar for my fourth groom to walk down the aisle and join me on the winding road of life, I heard Nanna's voice: "You're never alone."

Six hours later, after everyone had gone home and the pastor asked if I wouldn't mind leaving since he had evening services to conduct, I walked away from that altar. Was I wondering where my husband-to-be had disappeared to? No. I simply muttered to myself, over and over and over, "You're never alone. You're never alone. You're never alone."

❧

Death & Dying

LIVING WITH LOSS

$\mathcal{M}$y cousin Manny came to live with us when I was eight years old. His parents, mom's sister and her husband, had both recently died from injuries related to a train wreck. A cargo train carrying canned goods had jumped a rail outside of town, and Manny's folks were among those who instigated the looting. Later, they enjoyed the spoils, splitting a can of beets after they were sure Manny was asleep. But the can was dented, the beets tainted. By morning, Manny was an orphan. This strange twist of fate left my cousin alone, but it also left him with wisdom beyond his years—wisdom that helped me get through a tough loss of my own.

All my life I wanted a pet of my own, but dad always said life on a farm was no life for an animal. Perhaps he was right, perhaps not. I was never one to question my father's wisdom, but when Manny suggested dad's dairy could dramatically increase production if only he'd purchase a few cows, well, I couldn't question that either. I just wanted a pet.

I plead with my parents: A horse? "No," dad said, "it costs too much to feed." A dog? "No," dad said, "they shed." A cat? "No," dad said, "your mother hates cats. When she was a girl, her parents' basement was overrun with rats the size of small camels. The family cat turned and ran for its life. They lost everything."

"How about an indoor pet?" Manny suggested. "You know, like fish or a hamster or something you can keep trapped in a glass box on a shelf?"

Dad couldn't find a reason to say no, and that very afternoon we drove into town to pick up a hamster of my very own. The weeks that followed were the happiest of my life. Each day I'd jump out of bed to see what "Hammy" was up to. I'd sneak into the kitchen and steal the freshest lettuce for my little friend, then watch for hours as he wandered the tubes of his Habitrail. At night, I was lulled to sleep by the steady squeak, squeak, squeak of his exercise wheel. Then, less than two months after I brought him home, disaster struck: Hammy turned suddenly ill.

Luckily, Doc Penshaw, the local vet, was a hamster expert. I put Hammy in an old shoe box and Dad, Manny, and I jumped in the car and were off to Doc Penshaw's in a shot. The old veterinarian greeted us at the door—mom had called ahead—and he took Hammy directly to the examining room. He set the box on the cold steel of the examination table and opened the lid where Hammy lay dying in his bed of torn newspapers.

After a few minutes watching the old vet poke and prod my beloved pet, my dad asked him, "Does it look bad, Doc?" I was unable to speak.

"I'm afraid it's worse than that," Doc said, then he turned to me. "Son, I don't know what's wrong with your little friend, but I do know this: he's not a hamster. He's a gerbil. Ain't nothin' I can do for a gerbil."

I began to sob uncontrollably as Dad gave Doc Penshaw the nod to go ahead and do the only humane thing: to put little Hammy down. Manny took me into the waiting room while Doc and my dad tended to the unfortunate business ahead of them. Manny just held me, not saying a word, and when we heard the inevitable "thunk!" of the ball peen hammer coming down on Hammy's suffering, he held me tighter as I sucked in the strength not to cry any more.

"Life's tough, Cous'," he said. "You have to go with the breaks; you can't fight 'em. You have to turn everything over and look at them from the bright side."

"The bright side?" I sniffled.

"Sure. Things could be worse. At least there's more dark meat on a gerbil."

He was right, of course. Years later, when my folks died, Manny was there for me again. After the funeral, I took him out to dinner to say thanks. We split a bucket of chicken and looked to the bright side, and as I raised a thigh to my mouth I thought of Hammy and my folks and how the summer my cousin came to live with us was the best summer of my life.

☾

STARING DEATH IN THE FACE...

...AND TELLING IT TO BUGGER OFF

$\mathcal{D}$ylan Thomas said, "Do not go gentle into that good night./Rage, rage against the dying of the light." I say he was a wimp. Death sucks and reincarnation blows. I'm staying right where I am, I kid you not. I'm going to live forever, and I don't mean metaphorically like in the cheesy song, hoping I'll be remembered by some future goofus who's memorized the names of lesser-known twentieth century writers.

No, damn your eyes, can't you see, I'm going to be right here to kick that goofus's butt and spit in his face. I'm not just raging, I'm going in with body armor, guns a-blazin', and I'm not taking prisoners. I'm going to rip Death's head off with my bare hands and scream a barbaric "YAWP!" down its neck. I'll chew my own legs off and eat my fellow passengers on the boat crossing the river Styx, 'cause I'm not gonna go. The night ain't good, and the tunnel of light can bite me.

And I'm not just blowing hot air here, I'm stocking the bunker. I donate my own blood to my own private blood bank. I don't drive during rush hour, I don't cross the street, and I don't fly. I live in a sterilized house in the country a thousand miles from the nearest fault line or nuclear target. I grow all my own food hydroponically underground.

My fence is electrified and my dogs eat only raw meat. I've got the proper permits for my guns.

The refrigerator is loaded with black market organs for transplant, because I'm not going on any waiting list. I'm prepared to have my body cryogenically stored for future thawing. I've had virus-stopping filters surgically implanted in my nose. I've got nanotechnology robots in my blood vessels scraping out cholesterol. I'm cloning whole-body replacements in the basement, just waiting for a brain transplant if this body is damaged beyond repair. I'm going to have my consciousness uploaded onto CD-ROM as a backup. I've got an android duplicate of me in the back room.

I'll survive world economic collapse or the people of color finally overthrowing The Man. I'll hold on until the whole stinking planet is one big landfill, and then I'm out of here, I'm on a space station, a moon base, Martian colonies. I'm going to watch the sun go nova from a spaceship warping out of the solar system. If the Big Crunch is coming, I'll have found an alternate dimension where the universe is open-ended and infinite.

Who's coming with me? If you've ever used the phrase "Sure, the monkey was coughing up blood, but he was so cute I just had to pet him," don't bother getting your shots. Otherwise, hop on and play safe. Welcome back, my friends, to the show that never ends. Go to the bathroom, grab your bag, and we're on the road. Come on, let's go, I've got things to do.

☾

I Like to Think . . .

I like to think of those that have
passed on not as dead and gone,
but as merely off on vacation,
or perhaps just taking a long nap.

Of course, it's a vacation they'll never
return from or a nap from which
they'll never awake, and even if they
could, it would be really awkward
spending time with them after
they've decomposed for a while.

MISSING AN OLD FRIEND

He was irritating, and it got to me, I suppose. Mostly, I think it was his attitude: he was just plain insubordinate. He never listened to me, always looked away when I spoke to him, and refused to clean up after himself. He never respected me or my space. I never thought I'd miss him when he died.

I met him back in '78. We hit it off right away, developed a sort of trust. He needed a place to stay and I needed a roommate, so he moved in. But maybe it was too soon. That trust slowly disappeared, and eventually I found myself watching my back constantly. I couldn't tell you how many times he smarted off to me, how many times he ate the leftovers I was saving for myself.

It got to the point where I couldn't take it any

more. Something had to give, and it wasn't going to be me.

Well, I never did give. I snapped. One day, after coming home once again to a messy apartment and an empty refrigerator, I lost it: "Enough is enough," I yelled. "Get in the car. We're goin' for a ride."

It was a cold, dark night, the kind of night your mother never let you go out in when you were a kid, a good night for trouble. We got in my Gremlin and drove down to the river, where I confronted him. We argued briefly, then began to fight. We struggled for a bit, but I had him by weight and reach. I didn't mean to kill him. He jumped me and I just heaved him off, headfirst over the bank. I'm sure he must have died as soon as he hit the shallow, murky river bottom. But like I said, I never meant to kill him. It was an accident. Honest.

But as I drove home I realized that he had never really meant that much to me, and that I wasn't even sorry about ending his life. Sounds callous, right? Coldhearted? Maybe so. But then, you didn't have to live with the irritating SOB, pardon my French. But now, looking back, I do kind of miss him. His irritating ways have become endearing traits through the filter of time.

But he's gone, and I'll never be able to replace him. There could never be another one like him. I mean it. Really. They simply don't make pet rocks anymore.

☾

BUDGEE'S GREATEST GIFT

I remember waking up to a strange silence in my room. In my ten short years on this earth, I had never heard such quiet. Before my older brother moved out, I went to sleep and woke up to the sound of his ever-present transistor radio playing either the top forty hits or static in the middle of the night after the station had signed off. The very day he and his transistor went off to college, I went with my mom to the pet shop to pick out Budgee, a yellow and green parakeet.

He never turned out to be the kind of bird I had hoped for: one that would step onto my finger and let me pet his head with my finger. Budgee never wanted to be touched. But he helped replace my brother's absence, and each night I fell asleep, and each morning awoke, to the calming sounds of his squawking and nervous chatter—a gift I was never able to repay. But that, however, wasn't Budgee's greatest gift.

That morning of cold, dark silence came three years after Budgee arrived into my life. I slowly pulled the covers from my face and looked around the room. Everything looked normal. Clothes lay strewn about in their usual fashion; model car parts cluttered the desk and the floor beneath it. The window shade, its white surface obscured by monster car stickers, was pulled to the window sill and the morning light was just beginning to filter in around its edge. Budgee's cage was hanging in its usual spot and the seeds and feathers below the cage hadn't been disturbed. The bookcase looked just as it did any other morning— Wait a minute! Budgee was not on his perch!

I threw the covers from my Roy Rogers pajamas, sprang to the floor, and raced toward Budgee's cage, pausing briefly to remove the Lego that had lodged itself in my foot. My forehead pressed against the thin cold wires as I peered into the cage. There, on the floor of the cage with his feet in the air, lay Budgee.

I reached my hand into the cage and gently grabbed hold of my parakeet's body, amazed that he let me touch him. After figuring out an angle that accommodated both his body and my hand, I removed

Budgee from the small cage door and blew the flecks of bird droppings and seed shells from his feathered back. I crossed to my desk, brushed the model car parts to the floor, and laid Budgee on a tissue.

I quickly grabbed my brother's graduation picture from the wall, dismantled the frame, removed the glass, and held it over Budgee: if the glass steamed up, Budgee was breathing, alive. But his stiff legs wouldn't allow me to place the glass near his beak, so I picked up his body, angled his head into the glass, and gazed intently at the glass. No steam.

After what seemed like an hour, there was still no steam. He was definitely not breathing.

I felt my stomach sink. I set the glass on the desk and petted Budgee's head with my finger. If I stroked him just right, it looked as if his beak was talking, so I spoke for him in a scratchy, parakeet voice: "I'm not dead; I'm just in a deep sleep. Leave me alone." But I knew he was dead, and a solitary tear made its way down my cheek. Respectfully, I set his body back on my desk and covered it with a sock.

I slowly made my way downstairs to the kitchen. A note on the table said that my parents had gone to the store, so I had to make my own breakfast. I didn't feel like eating, but out of habit I opened the refrigerator door and took out the brick of processed cheese and a loaf of white bread. After first removing the crust, I stuffed an entire piece of bread in my mouth and commenced pushing it repeatedly back and forth on the roof of my mouth with my tongue. As always, I was trying to emulate my Grandpa Mike, my favorite person in the world and once the best duck decoy carver in the county. Since Grandpa died, I always tried to eat, like him, without the benefit of teeth.

The bread, however, did little to distract me, and soon my eyes welled up with thoughts of Budgee, now stiff with death. As I stared at the brick of cheese before me through teary eyes, it seemed to to take on a familiar shape. Inspired, I reached for a paring knife, poised it over the processed dairy product, and readied myself to create:

I cut the cheese.

Soon, with the knife and my bare hands, I had shaped a chunk of the gooey yellow cheese into an effigy of Budgee. But no matter how long I worked, the cheese never quite captured my parakeet's spirit. Frustrated, I stuffed another crustless piece of bread into my mouth and sat back. Then, with thoughts of Grandpa Mike's toothless grin encouraging me, the idea came. I grabbed my cheese sculpture and paring knife and ran up to my room.

I split Budgee's belly with the knife, removed his little organs, and arranged them neatly on my brother's graduation picture. Then I placed the shaped cheese into Budgee's feathered shell and closed the incision with model glue. Finally, with little ceremony, I taped him to his perch, where he still sits today.

When my parents arrived home from the store, I told them of Budgee's passing and showed them my handiwork. They were amazed at how lifelike my cheese-stuffed pal still looked and encouraged me to pursue my new hobby.

Today, twenty years later, I run the most successful and respected taxidermy businesses in the upper Midwest. My workshop is graced with a photo of Grandpa Mike as a boy of ten, holding the first duck he ever carved. And above my workbench, in the cage we brought him home in when my brother left for college, Budgee sits perched, overlooking my work.

In life he was just background noise. In death, he inspired me to greatness. Truly, his unfortunate passing was Budgee's greatest gift.

☾

Attitude

A Lone Dog Barks

*I*t was a dark and stormy night.

Not really. I've just always wanted to start a story that way. Actually, it was a warm, sunny autumn afternoon. A light breeze danced leaves of gold, orange, and crimson through the air. The sky was silky blue except for a few wisps of cottony clouds that floated peacefully above the richly colored trees that ribboned the horizon. A lone dog barked in the distance.

Suddenly, the breeze changed to a wind. The warm air turned cold, and dense black clouds unrolled themselves like a giant sleeping bag. The trees were blown bare and their branches shone like bent black skeletons against the strobe of the white lightning. Thunder crashed and echoed over the hillsides. A lone dog barked in the distance.

Turns out it really was a dark and stormy night after all.

What can we learn from this? Perhaps that, given enough time, the weather will change and day will turn to night, and maybe that's a metaphor: in other words, the good times don't last forever, or maybe the bad times aren't as bad as they seem and will eventually end. In either case we should be prepared for change no matter if things are good or bad. Maybe not. At least we can take comfort in the knowledge that lone dogs bark no matter what the weather.

A SMILE IS JUST A FROWN ON PROZAC

OR "EXCERPTS FROM THE MINUTES OF THE PROCEEDINGS
OF THE BISEMIANNUAL CONFERENCE OF THE COUNCIL
ON ATTITUDE CORRECTION AND ALTERATION"

. . . $\mathcal{P}$rof. H.M.S. Twiggins of Oxford has the floor. . . . [He] contends that the vernacularization of psychological theory and nomenclature has transformed psychiatry into a mythlike construct of popular generalizations that is rapidly losing all legitimacy and therapeutic value. . . . [To this end] he addresses Dr. Loretta Dobbs of Yale: "My professional opinion of this neo-Jungian, expert-on-a-chat-show prattle of yours is that I don't give a flying rat's ass shish kebob."

Dobbs strongly disagrees, suggesting that the proper application of one of the auditorium's chairs to the professor's "misshapen skull" might "wake [him] up for long enough to realize that Freud is still dead". . . . As several graduate students wrestle the chair away . . . Twiggson begins pelting her with cigars . . . apparently producing them from within the front of his pants. . . . A general scuffle ensues, but . . . things quiet down as Dr. Herby Scuttle, president of the Council and author of the groundbreaking work of existential psychoanalysis, *Neither of Us Is Okay*, takes the microphone to deliver the closing lecture.

The paper, entitled "Embrace the Hate Like You Would an Old Friend," is meant to address the concept that neuroses are not inherently bad, ethically or psychologically. . . . [Hence] neurotics are not necessarily "patients" who must be "cured". . . . [T]he audience, however, already decisively split along sensitive anal-oral lines, seems to take offense . . . and by the third page small skirmishes erupt. . . . Soon the battlefront spills into the rest of the convention center, involving a gathering of Amway distributors.

. . . After riot police clear the building, the implications of the weekend remain to be pondered. . . . [I]n the end, if you walk on the sunny side of the street, you'll always be as right as rain. There is, perhaps, a sense of affirmation when, later, Dobbs and Twiggins are discovered *in flagrante delicto* in a janitor's closet with a fruit basket and a concertina.

♭

It All Depends On...

*A*s a child, whenever I was frightened
by something, a trip to the
dentist or my first day of school,
my mother always said:
"It won't be so bad. It all depends
on how you look at it."

As an adult, I still find comfort in
mother's words, and whenever
I'm in a frightening situation,
I squint or even close my eyes.

And she's right: most problems
really aren't so bad if you can find
some way to distort or ignore them.

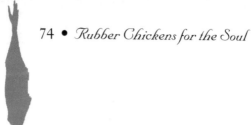

THE LUCKY LEOPARD SKIN

My Uncle Irv died last year and willed to me his leopard skin. It had once adorned the floor of his den, and I remember playing on the thing when I was a kid. Uncle Irv called it his "lucky leopard skin" and told my sister and me stories of how it had saved him time and time again. We never believed his tall tales, but we had fun with our contests to see who could guess how many spots were on the skin. Of course we never knew the actual number, and we always guessed in the millions. While I had warm memories of playing on the leopard skin rug, I didn't appreciate receiving it as an adult. My husband, "Mr. Politically Correct," wouldn't allow it in the house, it was inappropriate for my office, and I couldn't bring myself to simply stick it in the garage.

Eventually I just threw it into the back of my Civic, where it landed with its head pointed as if it was looking through the back window. One night my usual route home from work was under construction. I lost my way on the detour and soon found myself in an unfamiliar part of town. I tried to remain calm and find a way out quickly, without stopping, but I unfortunately encountered a red light.

Two cars with tinted windows pulled up on either side of me. The windows rolled down slowly to show both cars packed with seedy-looking characters wearing gang colors and sporting bad attitudes. I prayed for the light to change before they noticed me: I knew the Civic couldn't outrun them.

The light seemed to last forever. About a dozen dangerous young men got out of the cars and converged on the Civic. Some jumped on the hood, the rest surrounded it. One, the biggest, meanest-looking man I've ever seen, motioned for me to roll down the window. Reluctantly, I complied.

"Whatcha doin' on our turf, lady?" he said. The tone of his voice alone seemed to threaten my very existence. "What? You gotta death wish?"

The gang bangers moved even closer to me, and as their leader reached in to, I assume, pull me out and kill me, I heard someone shout, "Wait! You guys, look at this!"

They all stared into the back window, then slowly moved away from the Civic and back into their cars. As he walked away, the big one looked my way and nodded with what I imagined was respect. With no explanation, they revved their engines and drove away, leaving me, the Civic, and the leopard skin in a cloud of blue smoke.

Still too shaken to drive, I sat as the light changed back to red. As the exhaust smoke cleared, I could read the graffiti that covered the walls of an adjacent alley: "Leopards Rule!" it said, in large black- and orange-spotted letters.

It turned out that Uncle Irv's lucky leopard skin was a pretty darn good gift after all, and it has never left my car. Without it I may well have been killed for trespassing on the turf of the Leopards, the toughest gang in the city. Truly, it had saved my life.

From that day on I believed the stories Uncle Irv had told us when we were children, except maybe the one about Bigfoot and the Queen of England.

§

Eclectic Wisdom

Leaving Home

When I left home, I looked forward to the freedom of living on my own, not to mention the added privacy. After all, I was twenty-seven and I still spent what my father called "way too much time in the bathroom to be good for you!"

When the day finally arrived, dad woke me early, helped me pack, and even paid a buddy of his to help things go faster. My mother, on the other hand, just sat on the porch and occasionally murmured something about "abandoning" her.

With the U-Haul packed and dad leaning on the horn, I walked up to her to say so long. She offered no kiss good-bye, no hug, not even a little cash for groceries. She just stared at her feet and said, "I hope you're happy."

I walked slowly to the car. I hated to leave, but the time had come. It saddened me to leave her in such a state. Then, as I opened the car door, I heard her voice call to me: "Angelo!"

"Yes, Mama?" I called back.

"Don't ever cut lettuce with a metal knife," she called, encouragingly. "It'll turn brown, and then where will you be?"

I just smiled, waved, and got in the car. And as we drove off to my new apartment and a new stage in life, I was consoled by the wisdom she had imparted to me. Thanks to Mama, I was going to be okay.

❧

To Live Is To . . .

To live is to learn;

To learn is to live;

Careful!
The plate is really hot.

> — traditional proverb of
> Mexican restaurants

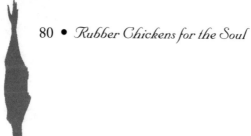

THE TRUTH MAY HURT,
BUT LIES ARE WORSE

I truly believe in the title of this essay, and I felt that way before I found out what's really going on out there. It's a good thing, too, because otherwise the enlightenment would have driven me insane. Instead, I embraced the ugly truth, happy to know it, glad to be relieved of the lies of appearances. If you'd rather keep believing what they taught you in school, that the United States of America is free, that Oswald shot Kennedy, that NBC canceled the original "Star Trek" because of low ratings, then turn the page and skip to something easier for you to handle. If you feel the way I do, if you think you're up to facing cold, hard facts, then read on.

Welcome, truthseekers. I guess I'll never know if

there was a causal relationship between the accident and my awakening to the truth woven into the fabric of our society. Maybe it was just a coincidence, but then what explains my sudden insight into what had always evaded my understanding before? I think the blow to my cranium stimulated some neurons and fired some synapses that had before lain dormant. It was as though lightning cut through a starless night sky, illuminating the landscape for the first time. And I knew.

As the passing rusty green Pacer kicked up a rock that glanced off my temple, spun my head like I'd caught a glimpse of a rare bird, and timbered me to the concrete like a lumberjacked tree, *I knew*.

The government is growing our clothes, and I don't mean cotton. They've got genetically engineered, alien DNA, irradiated plant/animals that grow clothes whole like blossoms and fruit. They just pick up the pants and shirts and what have you after they fall off "naturally." Why don't they reveal this miracle of modern science to the general public? Because the clothes are *still alive* and they see and hear everything we do.

You know the old saying "It all comes out in the wash"? Well, it does. But the fluoridated, chlorinated, chemically treated water we have has transformed the whole waterworks into a computer memory bank. Forget the phone police — they only hear what we say on or near the phone. Unless you're a nudist, there's not much you do without clothes or sheets around you, and it's all in the H_2O. So the next time you drive by a water treatment plant just think about that. Government officials are in there downloading your secrets from the water onto CD-ROMs to be sent to the climate-controlled warehouse hidden deep beneath Mount Rushmore.

Now, go on with your life. Rejoice in your knowledge, which is always better than ignorance. And remember, go naked as often as you can, and dig your own well.

◦

THE MEANING OF LIFE

*W*hat's it all about, you ask? What's the meaning of life, the combination to the safe that holds all the answers to who and why and what we are? Some say it's different for each of us. Some say we'll never know until it's too late. Some say the question's too vague in the first place.

Well, we say different. We know the meaning of life, and after all the centuries of debate and hubbub over various philosophical and theological schools of thought, it turns out the answer has been with us all along. It's so simple, in fact, you will wonder why you haven't already thought of it yourself, or at least why no one else has thought of it before. You'll kick yourself when you realize just how simple it is.

Let's get right to the point. The meaning of life is

Sorry!

Have to stop things here or we risk going over 33 ⅓ stories. As it is, we're kind of pushing it with the bonus chicken soup recipe on the next page. And, hey, don't go complaining. Did you really expect to find the meaning of life in a cheesy little humor book?

Bonus!

OUR FAVORITE RECIPE
FOR CHICKEN SOUP

- Combine soup and one can of water.
- Stove: Simmer, stirring occasionally.
- Microwave: Use a microwave-safe bowl. Cover; microwave on *HIGH* 3 minutes or until hot. Stir.

$\mathcal{N}$ow that's good eatin'! But remember to open that can first! We'd like to thank the good folks at Campbell's Soup for sharing their world-famous recipe. It's our favorite, and we bet it's yours, too. Of course, those of you watching your health might want to check into sodium levels in canned soups and other processed foods. According to the *Nutrition Action Healthletter*, some "regular" canned soups are "brimming with salt." They may not be as good for you as they are good to eat!

THESE BAD DOG APPAREL ITEMS SHOW YOU HAVE:

A. A great sense of humor
B. Great taste in humor books
C. A limited wardrobe budget
D. A limited wardrobe
E. All of the above

Top Quality Bad Dog Humor Apparel

WHERE DYSFUNCTION MEETS FUNCTIONALITY

SMILE FROWN PROZAC *tee*
#RCS001

GET ME A BEER
tee #RCS002

COOL BAD DOG STUFF
Your life won't be complete without these quality BAD DOG items.*

Completeness of individual lives may vary

BAD DOG MUG
#BD003

SAVE HUGE BUCKS ON A LITTER OF FOUR BAD DOG MUGS #BD004

Back of mug says:

I ❤ MY BAD DOG

Cap Back Design

BAD DOG CAP
#BD002

BAD DOG LOGO *Sweat* #BD001S
BAD DOG LOGO *T-Shirt* #BD001T

ORDERING INFORMATION

You can order by mail* or phone.
Fill out this handy order form prior
to calling so you don't forget anything.

_____ A Smile is Just a Frown on Prozac T-Shirt *(RCS001)*	. . . $17.95
_____ Get me a Beer T-Shirt *(RCS002)*	. . $17.95
_____ Bad Dog Logo T-Shirt *(BD001T)*	. $17.95
_____ Bad Dog Logo Sweat *(BD001S)*	. $27.95
_____ Bad Dog Embroidered Cap *(BD002)*	. $19.95
_____ Bad Dog Mug *(BD003)*	. $8.95
_____ Set of 4 Bad Dog Mugs *(BD004)*	. $25.00

XXL size t-shirts and sweats add $1.50
MN residents add 6.5% tax on non-apparel items
Allow two to three weeks for delivery
Shipping/handling charges: $5.00

Pick One:
☐ Free Button
☐ Free
   Bumper
   Sticker

FREE BUTTON
OR BUMPER
STICKER
WITH
EVERY
ORDER

Sub Total Items $	_____
Tax $	_____
Shipping Charges $	$5.00
Total $	_____

BAD DOG TOLL-FREE ORDER LINE
1-800-270-5863

VISA *MasterCard*

** To order by mail send your order with your name, address, phone
with a check or money order to:
Bad Dog Press P.O. Box 130066 Roseville, MN 55113*

DO YOUR BAD DOG SHOPPING ON-LINE:
http://www.octane.com

BITE INTO THESE OTHER

BAD DOG BOOKS

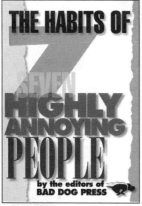

You know the type: they encourage mimes; they pass you on the highway and then drive too slow; they talk during movies; too often, they're your relatives. They're highly annoying people, and they play a much larger role in your life than do the highly effective.

Bad Dog's *The Habits of Seven Highly Annoying People* explores and exploits some of the most vexatious folks you'll ever meet. Great to give as an anonymous gift to people you find particularly annoying!

They call when you're in the tub. They call during dinner. They call when you're "reading" in the bathroom. And whenever they call, they try to sell you something you more than likely don't want.

They're telemarketers, and Bad Dog Press's latest offering—*How to Get Rid of a Telemarketer*—presents dozens of hilarious ways to help readers regain precious spare time free of senseless solicitation and leave even the most tenacious telemarketers speechless.

Perhaps you've never made the mistake of showing up for an interview wearing a tie that requires batteries or listing "donating plasma" under your résumé's employment experience section. Well, the authors of *Who Packed Your Parachute?* have, and they hope their book can help others to avoid making similar errors. Here is the complete guide to what NOT to do during a job search.

Who Packed Your Parachute is the perfect book for graduates, adult children living with their parents, and anyone else on a job search.

A WHOLE NEW BREED OF HUMOR BOOKS!

Like our namesakes, we at Bad Dog Press aren't afraid to dig in the trash, chew the furniture, or take off dragging the leash—but we do so with tasteful, funny books that will have you laughing all the way home from the bookstore.

As you read this, the folks at Bad Dog are busy preparing other books that you'll love! Watch your bookstore humor section for our latest releases.

HAVE A PEEK AT OUR FUTURE BOOKS!

Visit the BAD DOG Humor On-Line Web page to preview upcoming books, participate in fun contests, join in funny forums, and find out how you can contribute to future Bad Dog books. **http://www.octane.com**